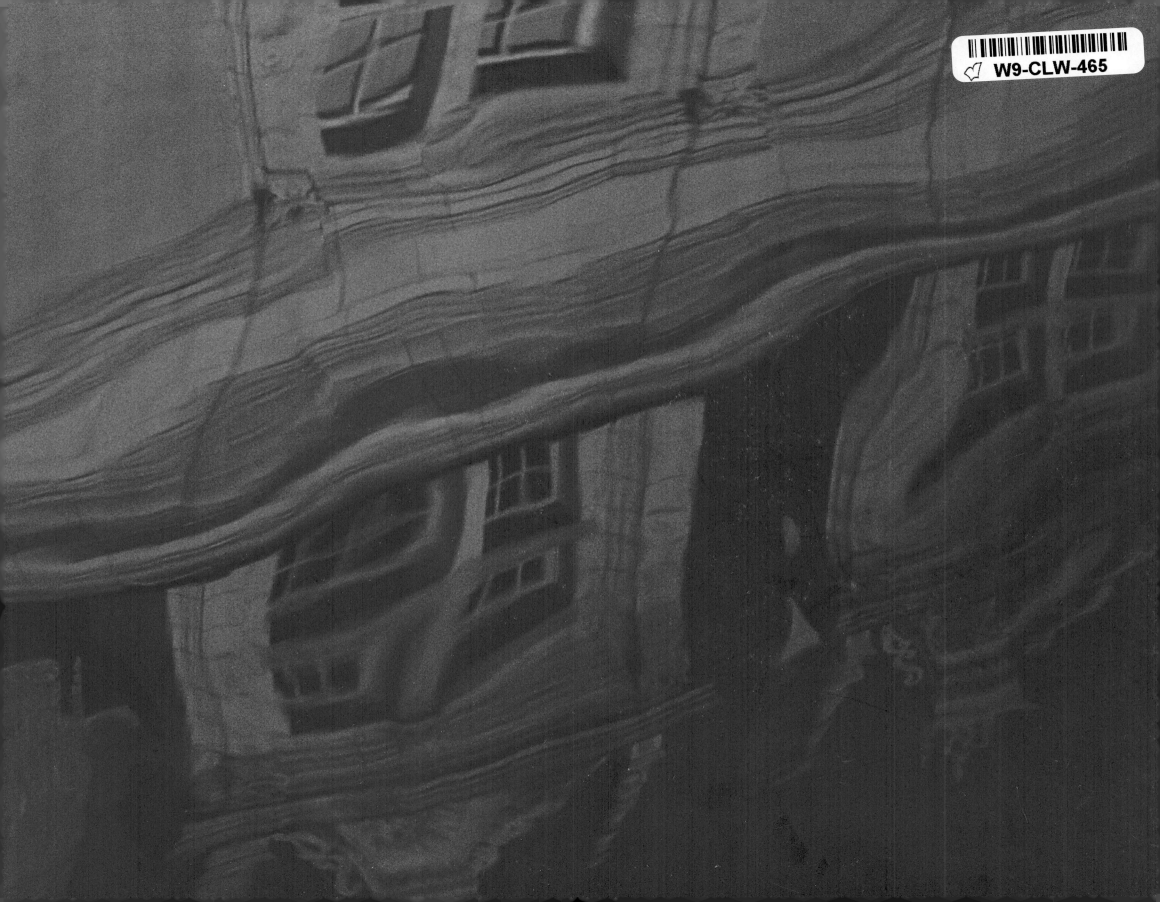

The Châteaux of the Loire

Original French title: LES CHÂTEAUX DE LA LOIRE, written by Pierre Miquel and photographed by
Jean-Baptiste Leroux. Published by Les Éditions du Chêne—Hachette Livre 1998.

Copyright © 1998, Éditions du Chêne—Hachette Livre

English language text translated from the French by Tracy Danison
Copyright © 1999 Éditions du Chêne—Hachette Livre

Pierre Miquel

Photography
Jean-Baptiste Leroux

The Châteaux of the Loire

PENGUIN STUDIO

Contents

Introduction

Building well—fort, castle, château—has a long history in the Loire Valley. In the last two centuries of the first Christian millennium, Viking longboats ranged the rivers of Europe. The realms of the Franks were not spared. Northmen—*Normans*—pillaged Angers, future kingly capital of Plantagenet and of Capet, set where the River Maine meets the Loire. Further east, they sacked Tours, where the rivers Cher and Indre broaden the valley, spiritual capital of Christian Gaul, and home to St. Gregory, author of the first *Histoire des Francs*. In those troubled times, Franks and flocks alike found shelter in wood forts built on the country's rolling slopes.

As time went by, pillage gave way to taxation and wood gave way to stone. Ruins trace a story of ceaseless petty wars, of robber barons and local potentates like Foulques the Red and Geoffroy Grisegonelle, and the medieval rivalries of the French and English royal houses.

The country around Tours, the Touraine, bears witness. At Langeais, just west of the city, are the ruins of a stone castle built in 994 as a base for collecting river tolls. Along the Indre, there is the formidable Loches, guarding access to the region from the south and Montbazon, lowering over the rich lands between the rivers. So too, in the country of Blois, the Blésois. North, along the River Brenne, which joins the Loire just above Tours, is Fréteval—where in 1194 the Plantagenet Richard the Lion-Hearted triumphed over the Capet Philippe II Augustus—and Lavardin, just below Vendôme. And so too, west and north, the country of Orléans, the Orléanais—famously delivered from the English invader by Joan of Arc in 1429, the beginning of the end of the Hundred Years War—the key to the Paris basin above. Below, there is Beaugency, the first way station, and above, on the River Loing, which fastens the Seine with the Loire, Châtillon-Coligny.

The English victory at Agincourt in 1415 made the English masters of France. The Capet kings were forced back beneath the Loire. In 1422, Charles VII, the *petit roi de Bourges*, the little king of the provincial town of Bourges in the south-central Berry country, also became the first *roi tourangeau* of France—king from the Touraine.

Charles built and fortified as needed in his embattled country. He loved living at fortress Chinon, near where the River Vienne meets the Loire and where the twelfth century had seen Eleanor of Aquitaine and Henry II Plantagenet staking the first English claim to France. He stayed long at Loches, *bête noire* of the English marauder moving up from the southwest. Loches—massive, impregnable—hardly a royal residence. But then royal is as royal does. Joan of Arc's decisive victory at Orléans no doubt allowed Charles's son, Louis XI, to be bored by it.

Louis was married at thirteen in the cathedral of Tours. He went to live at Amboise, above the city, toward the Blésois, on the Loire's southern bank. But his heart remained in Tours and the Touraine, with its vineyards rising in easy contours away from the river dotted with the sails of boats skipping along its slow course, an image of peace and prosperity. Tours, the richest city of the newly reviving realm of France. Tours, where France first found its history. It proved irresistible.

Louis bought land at Plessis to make his own royal seat, but the ongoing feudal struggle called for castles, not luxury châteaux. The towers of Plessis were as rough and impregnable as those of Loches. But to the city itself he brought Italian silk makers to soften the garments of prosperity, the remarkable glassmaker Jean de Paris to shed new light, and the painters Fouquet and Coppin de Delphes to teach the delights of the eye and mind.

It was left to the next generation to create the châteaux that we associate with the Loire, that reflect a taste for living rather than as a tribute to harsh necessity. Louis XI made feudal France safe for monarchy, acquiring Anjou and Burgundy. Charles VIII was weaned on the fruits of his successes. He led the first of what were to be many French incursions into Italy. When he returned to the Loire, he was no longer a man of the Middle Ages. For Charles, stone fortresses were prisons; he felt claustrophobic between walls two yards thick. He got moldy in windowless rooms. But worst, and best, of all, a mere castle bored him silly.

Charles found repose at Amboise. There he was born and

there he lived out a fortunate marriage with Anne of Brittany. It was impossible to knock down and rebuild its thick medieval walls and towers. Amboise was an extension of the bedrock it rose upon. But he could let the sun shine in, and add breadth to depth. That was the key to the beauty of Roman and Florentine *palazzi* and the marvelous *poggio reale* at Naples, to Milan's *Certosa* and the wide square that is graced by Michelangelo's *David*. He had seen the light flooding the uniform walls of the Pitti palace. The remarkable Flamboyant Gothic of the cathedral of Milan seemed a Baroque throwback when set against Ludovico Sforza's grand palace.

Charles's galleries, loggias, and flowers did not remake Amboise in the image of the Renaissance, but they opened onto it. Italy had taught Charles and his drunken cavaliers and all their descendants to love the light. Henceforth, it was possible to create a château, a fortress that made for both good soldiering and good living.

It was better to leave the medieval cities behind. Paris was just no good place to make a start on the new-found Italian plan. Neither was Lyons. Nor Tours. Narrow medieval streets could give no scope for the broad pavements and open marble façades of the churches of the Florentine-style piazza. The royal court began the Renaissance under the milky-blue skies of the Loire Valley under Charles's italianissimo son and grandson Louis XII and François I, who created the new shapes of the Renaissance with the châteaux of Chambord and Blois.

In this new ambiance, kings and courts set the standard of beauty and luxury. In the first decades of the sixteenth century, François I demanded that everything around him should reflect the image of the gods. His royal person dressed only in the silks of Milan and the velvets of Florence and Genoa. The works of art, the armor and cannons of war were gorged with gold. The halberds of his bodyguard seemed to be the work of sculptors, the rainbow hues of soldiers' uniforms the work of painters. Even the glasses and forks were of the Italian model.

It wasn't only ideas and silk that flowed from Italy. Duchesses now might be perceived sweeping—regally?—down the spiral staircases, while chatting earnestly with their poets and architects. Pierre de Ronsard, whose Pléiades circle renewed French poetry, wooed and wed the daughter of the Italian financier Salviati, met during a ball. And with the new money, the painters of portraits and frescoes, sculptors and architects from all lands were collected together with Flemish dyers and French masters in stained glass and tapestry. René, Duke of Anjou, also King of Naples, displayed the remarkable Apocalypse tapestry woven for his grandfather Louis I by Nicolas Bataille based on a design by the painter Hennequin of Brussels. The tomb of Leonardo da Vinci is at Amboise.

The boatmen of sixteenth-century Italy were sorely put to meet the demand for marble in the Loire Valley. Great flat-bottom barges with rectangle sails brought loads of Carrara marble to the quays of the Ponts-de-Cé at Angers and the port at Tours. From there, it spread through the country as sculpture, relief, façade . . . any elegant use at all. King René put gamboling deer in the moats of his fortress of Angers, thus humanizing the peculiar black schist and limestone inlays of its thick walls.

Once the ball was rolling, it was unstoppable. Every man or woman of power wanted space for living in all its new senses. Marguerite, sister of François I, welcomed dangerous Humanists to her court—the Gospels were read in French. The Protestantizing Clément Marot, sharp and sweet poet, valet to François I, was the guest of the Duchess of Ferrara.

All this was both a noble and common enterprise. The rising financiers dared to build if not in the image of gods, then in the image of kings. The château of Plessis-Bourré is the outward sign of the graceful munificence of Jean Bourré, a minister of finance; Chenonceaux, of Thomas Bohier, successful financier; and Azay-le-Rideau, the pearl of the River Indre, of Gilles Berthelot, treasurer of France and *richissime* mayor of Tours. In those days, châteaux and the new were the done thing. Even the royal secretaries were in on the act. Le Breton, aide to François I, created Villandry and Villesavin. Jean de Thier, secretary of state to Henry II, dared bring the poet Ronsard to Beauregard; the frolicsome sculptor Philibert Delorme did not disdain the job of drawing up the plan for Serrant.

Imitation may be the sincerest form of flattery, but imitation of kings could be costly. Thomas Bohier's son Antoine found it necessary to appease François I with the gift of Chenonceaux. But, for all the danger of tasteful *lèse majesté*, the kings created a style of life and luxury, a standard of beauty and charm, which would remain those of noble and commoner alike when they wanted to advertise their claim to distinction with a prestige château.

Le plus ça change, le plus . . . In 1900, France had 20,000 proprietors living in their châteaux. Many were still far from being droplets in the blue bloodstream, although, perhaps, they were chips off the old blocks, if less inclined to snobbery. At the end of the nineteenth century, Chenonceaux fell into the hands of a certain Lady Pelouze, née Wilson, the mistress of a wealthy industrialist and sister to a certain Daniel. Wilson became son-in-law to President Jules Grèvy, a founding father of the glorious Third Republic and former lover of Lady Pelouze, née Wilson. Daniel distinguished himself and honored his father-in-law by selling *légions d'honneur* and other favors in the presidential gift right out of the older man's office, thus authoring the Republic's defining scandal.

Grèvy might have done better if his Republican dignity had excluded the lady's regal entertainments. The great royal seat—and others—was the scene of vaudeville hilarities attended by upstart, be-muttonchopped, potbellied radicals showering their gallantries on *femmes du demimonde*. Daniel met President Grèvy and his daughter at one of these "dos."

Although the royal decor doesn't seem to have much bothered democracy's champions, their orgies did end the role of the château as a private showplace. As the Republic grew and then died and then revived, the immense white residences fell into disrepair, abandoned by fortunes exhausted by the wars of 1871, 1914, and 1939. As elsewhere in Europe, the state has had to pick up where individual resources have failed. After the ups and downs of a thousand years, royal luxury has entered the era of National Heritage. The whole world has become the heir of the châteaux of the Loire.

Fine round towers complement the faultless right angles of Gien's vast and comfortable living quarters.

Of bricks and slate: Gien

The châteaux of the Loire are at their most castle-like around Orléans, where the river sheers from north to west toward the sea. The region saw more than its share of war: the châteaux were built for troops keeping watch over the rafts of traders moving along and across the Loire. But three great sites dating from the fifteenth century show the symmetries of military necessity giving way to the softer line of better times and better lives.

Gien is French from bedrock up. The red and black bricks of its diamond-pattern walls are local clay, locally glazed. The gray slate clambering and curling up its roofs is from nearby quarries. The town that shares its name was a key to the heart of France—great in its time. Blessed with a bridge, coaches, and couriers striking from the royal seats at Fontainebleau and Montargis for the south-central Bourbon and Auvergne regions made the Loire here. So did merchants heading for the upstream towns of Briare and Roanne, where their goods would be carried on to Lyons, the jump-off for Renaissance Italy. Making the bridge made the town.

The château's sternest face, where the strong royal garrison bivouacked, towers above the houses and streets of the town as they step lightly down the high ground to the river's edge. It was here that France began its final, successful struggle against the English invader in the Hundred Years War. On March 1, 1429, Joan of Arc, fresh from counsel with Robert de Baudricourt, patriot Captain of Vaucouleurs, met Charles VII. Four months later, 12,000 soldiers were pouring in, determined to take Charles to Rheims and see him crowned. Victory for the House of Hugh Capet. Sacred history for France.

Then came new times and better lives. Anne of Beaujeu— Italian through her mother, Charlotte of Savoy, born in the prosperous and sophisticated Brabant, daughter of Louis XI and Regent of France—became countess of Gien. Anne loved the arts and *l'art de vivre*. As wife of the Duke of Bourbon, the lord of Beaujeu, she chose Gien as her residence. It straddled the road from Paris to Moulins, capital of the duke's ancestral seat. And from here she could carry on her mad

Gien's aesthetic essence is in its red and black bricks cradled in gray stone.

war against the Duke of Orléans, a feudal upstart and also the future Louis XII. In 1484, Anne and her brother, Charles VIII, dedicated Gien's humpback bridge of twelve stone arches. Royal favor had joined good fortune.

Favor and fortune are nothing without style. Anne used Gien's natural wealth of limestone, clay, and slate to rebuild the old château on a new, Italian-inspired plan. With its sharp right angles softened by fine round turrets, the château became a vast and comfortable space for living, but remained unfinished. A generation on, François I would find that its many windows and immense interior court gave ample scope for his entertainments and pomps. When, on August 11, 1523, he signed the act making his sister Marguerite Regent of France, the work Anne had begun was complete. More troubled monarchs found space enough for living here, too. In

1652, with aristocratic rebellion raging, Anne of Austria sheltered here with her infant Louis XIV, while the armies of the *frondeurs* Turenne and Condé ranged the country.

The château is today a museum of arms. Well-placed and wealthy, the site of a great deal of the ceaseless warmaking that has written France's history, Gien seems the logical choice for showing off some of the mechanics behind the terrors of battle. But the logic actually lies elsewhere. The only thumping hearts these crossbows, arquebuses, and flintlocks have stilled are those of the ducks paddling the Loire and the game abounding in the neighboring forests. These arms are the tools of the hunt—the ancient royal tradition, the undying peasant passion—not weapons of war. And the hunt abides at Gien even as the fanfares of history have passed it by.

*The many hues of Gien are
made more remarkable by the
seemingly esoteric figures
shaped into the brickwork.*

(Pages 22 to 25.)
Constructed on a limestone
promontory, Gien guards the
Loire as it turns west toward
the great towns and the sea. The
humpback bridge, the belltower
of the church, and the château
shape the horizon.

Fortress Sully

Sully, the first in the line of the *ancien régime*'s great statesmen that includes Mazarin and Colbert, took his name from this medieval stronghold at the northern tip of the Loire, originally a possession of the Trémoïlle family. The château's high walls and impregnable keep are reminders of its distinguished warrior past—Joan of Arc stayed at Sully during the Hundred Years War. It was a suitable choice for a man who knew a great deal of war and its fortunes.

Born Maximilien de Béthune, Marquis of Rosny, Sully began his illustrious life as henchman to the Protestant Henry of Navarre in the sixteenth century's wars of religion. Young Maximilien knew better than anyone how to take and hold a position, and distinguished himself as an expert in the science of fortifications. Such expertise was good to have when winning usually meant besieging and breaking sieges. And he had talents, too, at a time when soldiering was as much a test of manly enthusiasm and hardihood as of science.

Henry and Maximilien thought much of each other. Maximilien advised Henry to forswear Protestantism to gain the throne of France—he himself remained a Protestant. But "Paris is worth a mass"—so Prince Henry became King

Henry IV. Maximilien chose the sturdy old castle's name when Henry created him a duke and peer of the realm.

With a kingdom gained and a need to hold it, Henry naturally named Sully his grand master of artillery and fortifications, governor of the Bastille, and general superintendent of construction. Henry, one of history's eminently practical men, thought it best to name a rich man to manage royal finances; such a one would be less inclined to use the state's necessity to feather his own nest. Sully's marriage with the *richissime* Anne de Courtenay had given him a taste for managing money. Naturally, Henry named him his Superintendent of Finances.

Sully had character as well as talent. A man whose simplicity did reflect integrity, he rebuilt castle Sully as château Sully in the spirit of his own strength, right, and independence. He preserved the robust medieval core, but humanized it with a modern wing, the "little château" that today enfolds the Béthune tower in its gables.

The château became the consolation of a long exile. Henry died in 1610. At loggerheads with Marie de Médicis over her inspired largesse, Sully disapproved of a policy of aggressive Catholic Counter-Reformation. Feeling he was not able to

carry on the work he and Henry had undertaken, he resigned as a member of Louis XIII's regency council and withdrew to Sully.

Always dressed in a black doublet, awaiting death in disappointment, Sully quit the château only at his death in 1641. This statesman no longer expected reward, honor, or wealth from men. Rich and respected, a marshal of France, Sully swathed the château in the colors due to the great dead, welcomed few, and cloistered himself away. Sullen and irascible, he had no taste for livening up the austere architecture of his château with Italian novelties and passed it to his successors as he had received it—medieval and imposing, with a bare minimum of modern windows and accessible stairways. In those thirty years, he devoted himself to getting the happier times on paper as *Mémoires des sages et royales économies d'Etat de Henri le Grand*.

Château Sully remains of its time and of its owner. The Protestant cavalier defied the whole Catholic realm from its ramparts. Old-fashioned and massive, it is an anomaly along the upper Loire, the guardhouse to a Valley of Kings seduced by the charms of the Renaissance and the prestige of Italy, but has never been touched by them.

As the forest opens up,
the white mass of Chambord
peeps out from behind a detour
in a lane.

The folly of Chambord

Folie de grandeur, indeed.

All for parade. Chambord—fifteen years in the making, the fruit of the art of 1,800 masons. Unlived in, unlivable. All done so François I might receive Charles V—King of Spain, of New Spain, and of Sicily, Emperor of Germany and the Low Countries—in the sumptuous state that one inflated royal reserves for another.

Chambord lies snared in the loops of the River Cosson a bit more than a Gallic mile off the Loire on nearly 10,000 acres of woodland, where royal horsemen once ranged with ears anxiously cocked for the trot of wary deer. Its skyline speaks of fairy-tale enchantments. Three hundred and sixty-five chimneys poke through the autumnal mist along with innumerable spires and pinnacles dotted with light-shedding dormers. Closer up, round white towers roofed with fine gray slate dominate soaring façades. Within is a keep of four towers. Such an air of chivalric romance, but not an inch of the château is medieval.

The real Chambord lies within, structured around a monumental central staircase. Naturally lit from above by a transparent dome, the steps twist upward and downward like the proteins of the double helix. But it gives onto nothing and leads nowhere: from its highest reaches the adventurer has but a glimpse of a stone *fleur de lys*—six feet tall—fitted into the extreme point of a campanile. Chambord's bewitching skyline can be read as the roof of the world of deliberate enigma created within; amid a chimerical decor echoing Baghdad or Tibet, we can hear the Doge's ambassador to the Great King telling of the marvels and wonders of the East.

Although comparable to Versailles in sheer imaginative ambition—no king, great or otherwise, stayed long at Chambord. When its glory hour came it was an eighteenth-century *High Noon*, not *Henry V*. Under the gaze of the shaky Louis XV, mounted upon white steeds, Maurice of Saxony's volunteer Black Riders—Tartars, Turks, Croats, and Hungarians—performed a triumph for their master. Maurice was the victor of the Battle of Fontenoy, which won the War of the Austrian Succession, but was simply a prelude to the disasters of the Seven Years War (French and Indian War), which ended in the loss of most of France's overseas empire.

When the coarse huzzahs of Maurice's parade had died away, the silence of ruin fell over Chambord, only briefly,

tentatively, ruptured by the grunts of Marshal Berthier's loyal hussars in 1814, the year his Corsican tyrant's luck ran out. More tentatively still was the silence stirred in 1871—the year the Prussians strutted down the Champs Elysées and the Commune raged—by the irresolute machinations of the very Bourbon Count of Chambord, legitimist pretender to the throne. The state bought the place for 11 million francs from the Austrian Bourbon-Parmas in 1932. Just in time. No individual's wealth was equal to its upkeep. Even the Sun King wouldn't try.

It's hard to say from what Chambord sprang. A sketch of dreams by da Vinci? A vision of Pierre de Cortone, the master of the Baroque? There is some part of the phantasmagoria of the grand hunt in it, certainly. At Chambord, they say, Thibaud the Swindler, a tenth-century Count of Blois of damnable memory, has been set on an eternal nightmare chase as punishment for his sins.

Then there is romance, in the modern sense. Court ladies could serve up that kind of love at Chambord. They paraded beneath the gilded salamanders writhing in the caissons, gracefully tripping down the marble steps. The incredible

availability of concealed stairs, discreet corridors and nooks may have favored guiltier games. In a rage, Louis XIV smashed the window where François I had scrawled *Souvent femme varie, bien fol est qui s'y fie* (Woman is changeable and fool is he who puts his faith in her). As the balls and entertaintments rolled on, the discreet tryst within the crazy labyrinth becomes Chambord's glyph: an ephemeral meeting among hearts in love with enigma.

The vast tangle of spires,
towers, stairs, turrets, domes,
chimneys, and dormers
symbolize the spirit of fantasy
at Chambord.

*The profusion of towers large
and small, square and round,
thick and narrow finds a mirror
in the water of the little River
Cosson.*

Unlivable and unlived in, made just for parade, the phantasmagoria of Chambord is an exception among the lovely, but eminently practical, châteaux of the Loire.

La Pompadour's whimsy: Ménars

The original Ménars had the poker face of a state inspector of finances. Its builder, Guillaume Charron, was surely in its image. His grandfather had been post-horse keeper at Saint Dyé in the Orléanais. He was one of those seventeenth-century climbing bourgeois fattening a hard-won purse by lending money to the war-obsessed Louis XIII. Charron loved money and the Loire Valley. He had enough of each to make himself master-builder of his own castle. He had something more, too. It wasn't long before Ménars fell into the hands of Jean-Baptiste Colbert, Louis XIV's favorite economist and statesman and was soon created a marquisate. Colbert's wife, Marie, was Charron's daughter.

The château kept its stiff upper lip until 1760, when a woman of taste and *amour*, Louis XV's own Antoinette Poisson, Marquise de Pompadour, bought it and remade it in the image of knowing whimsy. La Pompadour was the Age of Reason's real minister of culture and first among its builders, as well as, it has been said, a big spender during the too-tender Louis's increasingly cash-strapped reign.

For all her *amour*, La Pompadour was a pragmatic and realistic soul. She first had the state build her a road to Ménars along the north bank of the Loire, eliminating the château's dependence on a ferry. To ensure rapid and secure communication with the court, she had the post-horse services transferred to Ménars. Her back taken care of, she then hired Jacques-Ange Gabriel as her architect. He, at the Pompadour's passionate insistence, had designed the Ecole Militaire at Paris as well as the Petit Trianon at Versailles.

Gabriel decided to keep Charron's austere residence, embellishing it with two separate buildings of a completely different style, enclosing a main court graced with a statue of the Emperor Augustus. After La Pompadour's demise, Gabriel's buildings were joined together by a gallery. This was the work of Abel Poisson, La Pompadour's brother and heir created Marquis of Marigny. It was designed by Soufflot, architect of the Panthéon.

But the real marvel is not inside the château, but the park outside. A double flight of stairs flows from the residence onto a terrace where we can admire Soufflot's orangery. Stretching out to the Loire is the *allée des Tilleuls*, La Pompadour's linden-spangled path to the Loire, where she strolled as she did and undid intrigue in the company of her many courtiers. Then there is the little temple of love. No doubt about it, Ménars was meant to be *Amour*'s leafy demesne. It is said that the traits of one of the griffins guarding the park wall represents those of La Pompadour.

As a whole, Ménars is both majestic: Charron's façade, and elegant: Gabriel's wings—a happy mix of the Louis XIII severity and Greco-Roman whimsy that dominated La Pompadour's time. It is a tribute to the strength of whimsy in a royal favorite who loved stone more than ballrooms and art more than life. While it is very much later, Ménars is in the same spirit as Chenonceaux and Azay-le-Rideau. Like them, it is an exception to the severe vastness of the buildings in the Loire's eastern reaches.

Having died in 1764, well before she had finished her *oeuvre*, La Pompadour was not able to make much of Ménars. But the château, passed from hand to inheriting hand, remains one permanent example of private patronage along the Loire.

A family home: Cheverny

Cheverny first existed as a medieval manor in 1510, built by a certain Jacques Hurault, a sturdy thread in Louis IX's robe of state. The blood and brick of the château have never been separated since—only Brissac can make a similar claim. And Hurault blood is as local as Cheverny brick: these were no mere Renaissance seekers of the sweet life. The family has been part and parcel of the Blois region since the fourteenth century.

Jacques, who became superintendent of finance, commissioner, governor, and bailiff of the county of Blois, wished to honor his prospering House with an ennobling home. The resulting castle—appropriate to a time when a man might still do his thrusting with a spear—was nestled into the valley of the River Beuvron, which meets the Loire just below Blois, on the ruins of an ancient winery.

The home that Jacques built was indeed worthy of his family. As was customary for members of the burgeoning corps of would-be *noblesse d'office*, scion Philippe Hurault made his fortune from the state. Chancellor to both the Catholic Henry III and the formerly Protestant Henry IV at a time when the country boiled with religious fevers and its noble lords had squared off in hostile factions, Philippe was an effective and faithful servant of a consolidating and appreciative monarchy. Created count by royal letters patent in 1577, Philippe then became the first chancellor of Henry III's *Ordre du Saint Esprit*, founded in 1578 and the most illustrious of the *ancien régime*'s chivalric orders. Philippe both came into and left life at Cheverny.

Scion Henry set about perfecting family history, finishing the common cloth of merit with a bit of soldierly mud in Henry IV's cavalry, thus putting a spur to the family claim of *noblesse*. This young veteran of the last of the wars of religion razed the old castle and built the modern château for his equally young wife, Françoise. Henry spent most of his time at a court known to be less than punctilious in matters moral, Françoise spent most of hers waiting at Cheverny, bored and uncomfortable behind weighty medieval walls.

Henry spared no effort to make an amusing and

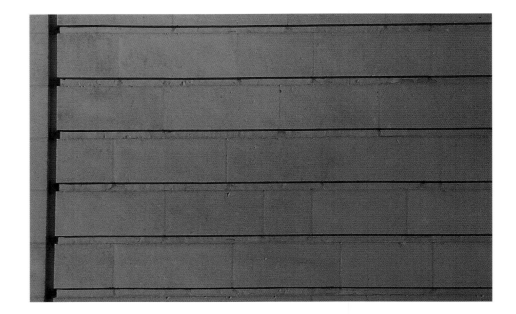

*Preceding pages: The back of
Cheverny is early sixteenth
century, while the front is late
seventeenth.*

*Twelve oval niches set between
the thirteen windows of the
south side shelter the busts of
Roman emperors.*

The boxiness and flattened domes of the roofs lend a monumental look to the flanking pavilions.

*Tradition says that the pavilions
once held apartments.*

The huge landscaped park around the château recalls the centrality of the hunt in Cheverny's life—past and present.

comfortable home for Françoise. The result was of noble aspect and of impeccable symmetry. Two tightly squared wings, domed in slate and topped by air- and light-giving lanterns, flanked a tall and narrow residence of elegant apartments. The wainscoting boasted gracious scenes of love and life and the majestically simple central staircase rose on sculpted panels.

Alas, disappointment, rage, and vulgar scandal exploded amid the magnificence. Returning one fateful morning at 5:00, Henry caught Françoise in the arms of a Burgundian gentleman. The irascible and jealous husband forced the guilty wife to drink poison. He had the Burgundian executed. Unfortunately for the cuckold's courtly ambitions, Henry IV heard of the affair. He thought the punishment of death considerably—by a century or two, even—exceeded the

crime of adultery, so he exiled the intemperate young man to Cheverny for three years. The *roi galant* hated nobles who made their own justice.

Coincidence might create the proofs of family memory, but then family memory might create coincidence. Each heir has added to the precious ornament of this home that became a marquisate: the theme of absence and fidelity, the exhilaration of hunting truth and the tragedy of paying it out, seem to bind them into a story. The seventeenth-century Aubusson tapestry depicts Paris's perfidious kidnapping of Helen of Troy; and the Gobelin, the story of Ulysses's wanderings. One of Henry IV's traveling cases is the rarest piece in the museum; we can contemplate the some 2,500 hunting trophies, proofs that at Cheverny, the prey has not always been elusive.

The royal portraits of
Beauregard

The Blois region, the Blésois, was Italy's port of entry to the Loire Valley. It lies beneath the broad bend where the Loire turns its waters from north to west, stretching from the western bank facing Gien toward the wonders of the kingly châteaux of Blois, Chambord, and Cheverny. Hunched above the town bridge of Beaugency, the feudal castle of Dunois plays gatekeeper to this bit of the domain of France, rich in fine wines, as well as sixteenth-century châteaux. To the south, in the heights above the little River Beuvron, brushed by the boughs of the forest of Bussy, stands Beauregard, a pure product of the Renaissance, as severe as any castle.

Beauregard has its Italian credentials. It was created in the mid-sixteenth century during the reign of Henry II, husband of the very Florentine Catherine de Médicis, for Jean du Thier, one of the four grand royal ministers. With an eye to the new aesthetic developing at court, he chose the Bolognese architect Sebastiano Serlio, who had first worked at Fontainebleau. Serlio was a cultured man of modern sensibilities, who in his turn hired the painter Niccolo dell'Abate, also a veteran of Fontainebleau, to swathe the chapel in Florentine-style frescoes.

Thier was a friend of the reforming and deaf poet Pierre de Ronsard, who took his cues from the elegant philosophizing of classical Greece and Rome. He intended Beauregard to be a sort of deluxe hermitage. Within, a statesman like Thier might lay down the cares of power for a while. These were growing more wearying as Henry's pursuit of the war against Hapsburg domination in Europe dragged on and on. When Thier inaugurated Beauregard in 1550, Henry had just taken Calais from the English. In the age of Machiavelli and religious ferments, statecraft could burden the spirit as well as the brain. Henry, a scion of very Catholic France, would later enter into shameless negotiation with the Protestant German princes against Spain's most Catholic Philippe II.

At the beginning of the seventeenth century, Beauregard had a master who changed its classical spirit of repose. Paul Ardier, comptroller general for war—financier to Louis XIII's Hapsburg War—never ceased altering Thier's hermitage. He added a pure, austere, square wing in Louis XIII style, but he was no man for sloughing off worldly concern. Significantly, his blue Delftware tiling shows Louis's army—the one that his loans were feeding—on the march. He brought in the Blésois painter Jean Mosnier to portray 363 historic figures. Notable among them were the kings of France from the thirteenth century's Valois Philippe VI to his own Bourbon Louis XIII.

Portraiture is a French genre, of course; could it be that all this obvious homage to the king was designed to distract Louis's harsh gaze from the insolent wealth of his own comptroller general for war? But Beauregard was off the main road so Louis never visited. Ardier loved the oak of the nearby forests, sculpting and gilding it for the panels that make the ceilings and, especially striking, for the bell cabinet conceived by the sculptor Scibec. Bells figured in the coats of arms of the Thier family. Included in the military themes of Ardier, they were a reminder that Beauregard had been raised up for the pleasure of the senses and the repose of the soul.

In the shadow of the forest of Bussy at the southern end of the Beuvron Valley Beauregard is a Renaissance creation remarkable for its sumptuous interior.

The alternating pattern of red
brick, slate, and white stone
distinguish the Louis XII wing of
the château of Blois.

The kings of Blois

The ominous but energetic Thibaud the Swindler, Count of Blois, built the first fort on the site of today's château in 978. The Châtillon and Orléans families developed the place into an elaborate castle. In the fifteenth century, the castle was rebuilt in brick and cut stone by Charles d'Orléans, who spent twenty-five years as a captive in England after Agincourt. He acquired a modern sense of comfort and luxury. Charles, who was a poet before becoming a famous father, married Marie de Clèves between rondeaus. The couple's issue, the rebel, then royal, Louis XII, was born here in 1462. Blois would become what the poet Pierre de Ronsard has called the "Repair of Kings."

Coming to the throne at the death of the heirless Charles VIII in 1498, Louis was the first of the Valois branch of the House of Capet. He built the royal residence dominating the interior court, signed his decrees in it, and lived in it. Anne of Brittany, the wife Louis married to prevent her Celtic domain from falling into foreign hands, died here in 1514. Their daughter, Queen Claude, brought her husband, Louis's cousin François I, down for a visit.

François added a wing and, with his customary splendiferousness, here received the Spanish-German-Italian king-emperor Charles V. The Valois embellished as often as they visited. François's son, Henry II, and Henry's son, child-king Charles IX, under the protective wing of his mother, Catherine de Médicis, were, of course, constant visitors. When the religious pot got boiling, Blois became a royal redoubt.

Henry III, the last Valois, retired here from ultra-Catholic Paris. It was to Blois that, in 1588, he called the Three Estates—nobles, clergy, and commons—together to look for a way out of the Protestant-Catholic war that ravaged the country. He wrecked his own efforts by instigating the assassination of the ultras's leader, the Duke of Guise, and his brother, the Cardinal of Lorraine, on December 23, 1588.

The bitter end of the seventeenth century saw the royal presence decline. The newly minted Bourbon Capet, Henry IV, stayed away from Blois, although his complex family life kept it busy after his demise. His son, Louis XIII, used it to imprison Marie de Médicis, his intriguing mother. It didn't work; the queen mother was too big for the place. She made an escape worthy of D'Artagnan. His brother, Gaston d'Orléans, who was always ready to contemplate setting aristocrat against royal, set up his parallel court here.

Gaston employed the architect François Mansart—of Mansard-roof fame, as well as the founder of French Classicism—to rebuild the château in proportion to his royal ambitions. Mansart wished to replace the extravagant Gothic and picturesque Baroque with the pure lines and forms of vast façades and perfect domes, but Gaston just had too many financial irons in too many political fires to give much shape to Mansart's vision. He did manage one wing, though. It ruined him.

Blois has been marked with the vision of each of its successive owners by many renowned hands. The late Gothic is from Colin Biart, who also dreamed his dreams in the lines of the château of Amboise. The Italian-style gardens are the work of the Neapolitan Pacello da Marcoliano. François I's arcades are the distilled Renaissance ambition of Domenico da Cortona. In the service of a man who would be king is the severe classicism of Mansart's wing. Among these great men from a world now very far away, it would be remiss not to mention one from a time closer to us. In the mid-nineteenth century, it was the genial architect-cum-renovator Félix Duban who resurrected the château, which had fallen into ruin, for Napoléon III.

Dazzling Chaumont

Chaumont began in the tenth century as a wooden fort built for Eudes I, Count of Blois. It became a medieval keep in the twelfth century, when stone replaced wood. The events of the mid-fifteenth century brought low its towers and ramparts. Its lord, Pierre d'Amboise, joined with the feudal nobility of the League of the Public Good in revolt against a strengthening monarchy. The victorious Louis XI punished Pierre's hubris by pulling his castle down, but the abasement didn't last long. In 1472, Marshal and Admiral of France Charles II d'Amboise was using Chaumont to receive Louis XII in pomp and circumstance. The now somewhat Gothic château was faithful to the spirit of the Renaissance it was reborn into: good enough for an Italian queen. At the death of her husband Henry II in 1560, Catherine de Médicis bought it.

The uses Catherine made of Chaumont say as much about her worries as her tastes. She invited the Florentine stargazer Cosimo Ruggieri to plot her celestial destiny here in the Astrologer's Tower. She provided its first prisoner, Diane de Poitiers, mistress to two kings. Unfortunately for her, one of them had been Henry II. Catherine forced Diane to exchange Chenonceaux for Chaumont, for Chaumont made Catherine restless. Diane sank into a listless old age here.

Much later, Napoléon used it to coop up Madame de Staël, another obtrusive female.

The Chaumont of today owes most to the nineteenth-century architect La Morandière, who rebuilt it along neo-Renaissance lines for the heiress of the Say sugar fortune. She and her young husband, Amédée, Prince de Broglie, were dissatisfied with the accommodations. So many illustrious guests, but so many uncomfortable guests! So, at the dawn of the Third Republic, the couple transformed the château into a modern home of dazzling comfort, magnificence, and luxury. Monsieur le Prince and Madame la Princesse made those golden sugar chests dance.

Chaumont had never before known such magnificence. The neighboring hamlet was razed and the park extended to 6,000 acres. They had the tiling embellishing the old guard room lifted piece by piece out of a palace in Palermo. Even the horse troughs were enameled. Along the garden's lanes of impeccably white sand, guests might admire the orchid collection. The center of attraction for a leisurely promenade was Miss Pungy, an elephant that Madame la Princesse brought back from a trip to the East Indies on her private steamer Victoria. Guests slept in rooms with electric light supplied by a private dynamo—in 1898. Luxury did not neglect entertainment. Amédée organized hunts with forty-two horses that were accompanied by fifteen equipages—carriers and servants with the paraphernalia of blood sport. His guests golfed in the park and dressed for the balls or shows provided by the Comédie Française and the Opéra de Paris that were engaged to liven up the evenings.

Say goodbye to all that. The Chaumont of marvels and frolics closed up shop with the sudden ruin of the Say sugar business. Miss Pungy found a new home at a zoo. In 1938, the state bought Chaumont for 1,800,000 francs, a mere bagatelle. It took a while, but Chaumont finally did give joy to a woman, albeit in Republican times and all too fleetingly.

In the nineteenth century, the ancient castle of Chaumont was completely restored in the neo-Renaissance style.

Rooted on a rocky promontory,
Chaumont soars proudly above
the little village at its feet.

My fortune, Montrésor

Montrésor is a link in a chain of fortifications that snake out from and around the impregnable fortress of Loches. Loches itself perches strategically above the valley of the River Indre, the southern route into the Loire Valley. The Indre joins the Loire just below Tours.

When it comes to war, history develops quickly. So from when in the misty tenth century Foulques Nerra, Count of Anjou, laid its stone walls, the list of Montrésor's medieval lords also became a list of victory and defeat. In the late twelfth century, Plantagenet Henry II received it from his father, who had received it from *his* father, William the Conqueror, as part of the English throne's French lands. The old fortress was a solid place, well endowed with ramparts and towers, but in the early thirteenth century, the Capet Philippe II Augustus captured it and ensured the ascendancy of the durable House of Capet on French soil.

Throughout the thirteenth and fourteenth centuries the lords of Montrésor were noble men of the sword, warriors like Pierre de Palluau, who was a prisoner of the English, or Jean de Bueil, whose lord lieutenant, La Dignolaye, ransomed and burned the baronial barns and manors of friends and enemies alike. La Dignolaye thought it wise to make Montrésor impregnable by erecting parallel defensive walls.

The king's peace developed during the middle of the fifteenth century, and the king's men took possession of Montrésor. However, it can be dangerous to handle the king's money. Imbert de Bastarnay was one of these new-order noble masters. He was counselor first to Louis XI, who was the sovereign lord of Loches, then to Charles VIII and Louis XII. Trouble came in 1527, when the regent Louise of Savoy accused Jacques de Beaune, lord of Semblançay and royal banker, of embezzlement. Many men of quality like Imbert proclaimed Jacques's innocence, but she nevertheless had him hanged from the gibbet at Montfaucon. Imbert, however, was true to the end, and refused to repudiate him. Thinking, perhaps, of Jacques's fate, Imbert had his own tomb dug in the collegiate church under Montrésor's walls. His effigy and those of his wife and son pray eternally, while the Apostles watch.

With the warriors gone, Montrésor did at least become livable, even if it didn't lose its crenellated towers. In Louis XII's time, mullioned windows were gouged out of the walls, while dormers with lancing pediments were installed on the gabled roof to let light shine in on a renovated interior. The old defensive towers on the south side, overlooking the valley of the Indre with their machicolations for pouring boiling oil or boulders on too-insistent visitors, were complemented with two fine turrets on the north side.

The church and château are pure examples of French Renaissance taste. There is no excess, no flippant decoration—just as Imbert's wife, Georgette de Montchenu, wished. It was she who had the oak doors and stalls ornamented with medallions made for the church. It was a time of religious renewal: all the decorations have as their theme the Passion of Christ. And if the light, air, and themes are perfect, the site is enchanting. The little slate-roofed village of Montrésor huddles around the château's feet, spreading out like an amphitheater on the northern side of the valley. Thus the fashion for the Italian made an elegant country seat from a rough fortress. As the wars and rumors of wars died away, good fortune allowed Montrésor's new lords, courtiers, and men of business a little terrestrial paradise to console them in more mundane cares.

Thomas Bohier built
Chenonceaux on the ruins of an
ancient mill.

Château of queens: Chenonceaux

Chenonceaux's history did not begin with a queen. The farmer-general Thomas Bohier began Chenonceaux in 1513 around a ruined keep and an ancient mill on the River Cher, which meets the Loire just below Tours. Bohier was married to Catherine Briçonnet. She was the daughter of the Bible critic and enlightened Bishop of Meaux. Bohier was the first in the valley to build on the Renaissance plan, renovating the old structures and adding a sumptuous new wing along the river. Bohier's handling of royal money was a tricky as well as a lucrative business. Bohier's eventual ruin brought in the queens.

The new château fell into royal hands. Henry II was the husband of Catherine de Médicis as well as the lover of Diane de Poitiers. He presented Chenonceaux to Diane, who thus became its first queen. Catherine would make sure that she would be the second. For the moment, however, Henry and Diane made the best of things. They brought in Philibert Delorme, the leading architect of the French Renaissance and builder of the original Tuileries palace, to embellish and ornament. He built a bridge to link the château to the other

side of the river along with two floors of luxuriously decorated and furnished royal apartments. Diane lived in them, as would François I. He also built the luxurious galleries that stretch sixty meters over his bridge, but under the queen-mother's direction. Henry died and Diane was forced out of Chenonceaux and into exile at Chaumont.

Catherine wanted to extend her successful building efforts further by creating a mirror wing for Chenonceaux on the opposite bank, but never had the time to put her plans in motion. With Diane languishing satisfactorily at Chaumont, Chenonceaux's classic lines and water theme were a lure for the queen's gorgeous fêtes for the rich and beautiful. Her talented hand—and she later engineered the Saint Bartholomew massacre—let sweet folly flow. One evening, her lovely halls saw Henry III appear in women's clothes surrounded by a gaggle of his mincing male favorites, and the party continued after Catherine went to rest. In 1560, Francesco Primaticcio, veritable director of beaux arts to the Valois courts, showered violets and fragrant wallflowers of welcome on the youthful François II and his new queen, Marie Stuart. The poets of the Pléiade, renewers of French verse, led by the illustrious Pierre de Ronsard himself, composed rhymes for the occasion. Statues had been made expressly for the feast, and the guests' costumes were part of the whole theme. It seemed that all the splendors of Italy had settled in the Loire.

The religious wars turned human comedy into tragedy. In 1589, the fanatic monk Jacques Clément mortally wounded Henry III, would-be reconciler of Huguenot and Catholic. The widowed queen, Louise de Vaudémont, came to Chenonceaux and swathed it in her mourning. The reign of queens at Chenonceaux soon ended.

Then the period of bourgeois men of finance and business began with the advent of the Dupin family. Times had changed, but the eighteenth century and its denizens also frolicked. The Dupin settled comfortably in the château and invited the gorgeous and great of the epoch to join them. Jean-Jacques Rousseau felt so pampered by the luxury that he said it made him "fat as a monk." The turbulence of the Revolutionary period put an end to the Dupin family's masquerade. Chenonceaux was abandoned until the mid-nineteenth century.

Enter the masters of reality. The Second Empire's railroad barons and factory dukes sought royal accommodation, and their itchy hands stretched out to grasp at an older magnificence. Lady Pelouze, the sister to Daniel Wilson, whose sales of presidential favors would make him the Third Republic's defining grafter, persuaded her industrialist husband to buy the château. To his credit, Pelouze saw the merit of being able to entertain his imperial-cum-republican contemporaries in traditional royal style, and President Jacques Grévy was among the guests. This sexagenarian lawyer from the Jura mountains was believed to be of rigorous moral scruple. But he showed himself so appreciative of Lady Pelouze's stylish hilarities that he saw fit to marry his only daughter to the indelicate Daniel.

Thus may the delights of queens fall into the hands of scoundrels.

*The Gothic chapel is visible
from the south bank of the River
Cher. Here queens heard Mass
within the heights of this special
place.*

(Overleaf) The Tour des
Marques *flanking the entry of
Chenonceaux is a remnant of
the original castle and its
owners.*

Guarding the road from Loches,
Montpoupon has kept all the charm of
those ancient castles transformed into
Renaissance châteaux.

The discreet charm of Montpoupon

Montpoupon sits on a bulging slope, overlooking a little valley. The road lies below in the shadows of the forest, cut here and there by the trails of wild boar. In ancient times, fortifications were built here, for traces of fifteenth-century construction attest to far earlier origins, where knights had to pass.

Like many other châteaux on the Loire, Montpoupon's history is almost totally lacking. It sits midpoint athwart the road between Loches on the Indre and Montrichard on the Cher. Montpoupon has no river of its own to stake a strategic claim, but its fortified walls watched over comings and goings at a time when the Loire's rough lords were always prompt to pick up a lance and head for the neighboring demesne. The medieval counts of Anjou used the road to bring their armies up against the counts of Blois.

Although the chief glory was gained at the ports and fords, the land in between was also important in this river country. Montrichard guarded river traffic on the Cher and the south ford above Montpoupon. Foulques Nerra, a ruthless eleventh-century count of Anjou, constructed Montrichard with three defensive walls wrapped around a three-story castle with walls three yards deep jutting over the whole region. The lords of Amboise held the stronghold in fief until the fifteenth century, when Louis XI broke the back of the Loire's feudal order, bringing unruly Anjou and Burgundy into the royal dominion. Loches on the Indre held the keys to the Loire Valley below Montpoupon, and Louis was master there. Montrichard was ceded; he wanted the Cher also.

Montpoupon's entrance is well fortified. Three towers pinion the rectangular pavilion that served as the lord's residence. Arrows, boiling liquids, and boulders could make unwelcome entry a very tricky business; access to the interior courts was through a door beneath battlements slashed with machicolation. Inside, a redoubtable-looking cylindrical keep was linked to covered parapets along which defenders scurried to mount the guard.

Montpoupon is unusual, for strong places at Gentillé and Corbery in the same area show no traces of similar fortification. When more mundane cares could be put aside, the stronghold made a good regular meeting place to keep the men, dogs, and horses of more innocent blood sport at the ready. In the sixteenth century, a bit of sculpted ornament came to dress the surly walls and crosses were cut in them to let in more light. Judging from the gray monochrome paintwork put on the walls around 1438, some special attention was given to the interior.

Like Loches, the Renaissance château of Montpoupon has conserved the charm of the medieval castle from which it rose. Looking out over the soft light and shadow of the valley evokes the times of shepherds and panpipes. Surely living was good at Montpoupon in the time when Charles VII, crowned and flush with the expulsion of the English invader, thought only of the pleasures of love.

One of two residential halls containing
royal apartments. The St. Antoine tower,
formerly the church bell tower, is in the
background.

Impregnable Loches

The castles of the Loches region were first and foremost
strongholds sited above the valley of the River Indre on the
southern rim of the Loire country. Below lay the royal
provinces of Marche and Limousin, notorious haunts of the
English pikeman-adventurer when the Plantagenets
contended with Capets for the heart of France. Whoever
embarked from the mouth of the Indre might reach northeast
to Tours and southeast to Angers. Bottled up in Eleanor's
Aquitaine, Plantagenet eyes never ceased to covet the
Lochois.

Rising from a low hill overlooking the west bank of the
Indre, Loches was the valley's principal stronghold when
France was still taking shape. Its walls and towers squat atop
a fortified Roman town. They once formed an ellipse two
kilometers in diameter within which villagers and their herds
and flocks could weather a siege. The south side, with a two-
tower keep whose brows remain formidably beetled despite
the wear and tear of time and fronting towers raised by
Henry II, is the most strongly fortified face of the castle. It

was difficult to take Loches. It remains one of the most impressive examples of medieval French military architecture.

France's first chronicler, St. Gregory of Tours, said that a castle stood here in the sixth century. Foulques the Red, a tenth-century count of Anjou, had later possessed it. His son, Foulques Nerra, made it his headquarters for his struggle against the count of Blois. Plantagenet Richard the Lion-Hearted captured it in 1194, only to be dislodged by Capet Philippe II Augustus in 1205. After Philippe's victory, Loches became a royal residence as well as a pivot of the realm; a thirteenth-century royal door with two flanking towers controlled the vast interior. In the early fifteenth century, Charles VII, the little king of Bourges, stayed here with his Lady of Beauty, Agnès Sorel. Here it was that Joan of Arc inspired Charles to take the road to a crown at Rheims and a liberated France. Charles's turbulent son Louis XI felt safe here. He used the cellars carved out of the living rock for torturing his political prisoners.

Royal residence added the first humane touch to Loches although it was still a medieval castle at the time of Charles

Loches is one of the most impressive examples of French military architecture.

The Roman-era keep.

VII and his Sorel. The embellishment that transformed fortress Loches into a château began toward the end of the fifteenth century. Louis XII cut windows and dormers on the castle's north side, thus brightening the living space. Above a magnificent porch made gay with sculptures, he added a loggia rising in three arcades. The dazzling luxury of his apartments is in stark contrast to the relative sobriety of those of Charles.

The rough old castle of Loches had other attractions that ensured, perhaps, that the Renaissance kings would open it up and nudge it toward a brighter present, even if they never erased or wanted to erase its warrior past. Philippe II Augustus had made it historic ground, and Joan of Arc had consecrated it. Ladies as fair and delicate as Agnès and Anne of Brittany, wife of both Charles VIII and Louis XII, found it a propitious place, worthy of the small chapel that Anne had built. Louis XI, enemies snarling and snapping at his heels, felt safer here close to the holy city of Tours, where he went to make his devotions, than at the Louvre in profane Paris. He hid out here while his faith healers strained to restore his failing health.

The château entrance.

The older residence is linked to the Tour d'Agnès Sorel by a narrow walkway.

*Crowning the slope of the River
Indre and its valley, the château
of Loches is a fortified town
within a town.*

The bloody denouement of the conspiracy at Amboise cast a grim shadow over this château beloved of Renaissance kings. Royal paradise became an aristocratic prison.

The quiet captain of Amboise

Amboise, Chaumont, and Chenonceaux lie at the core of the Loire Valley. Chenonceaux is pure Renaissance invention. Chaumont and Amboise began as medieval fortresses perched above an important river, and invention came later.

Clovis, sixth-century king of the Franks, whom France claims as its first king, had a fortress here. A little island splits and shallows the river here, so armies may ford. The Amboise spur blocks the road south and from its heights men may survey the river and control traffic. The high and martial Minimes tower sits directly on the Loire; the Hurtault tower is set just above its confluence with the little River Amasse. The spiral entry ramps are civilizing touches; they made the castle accessible by horse and carriage as well as by foot. Henceforward, one might come into Amboise as one might come into a palace.

Charles VIII was born here in 1470 and died here in 1498. He failed in his attempt to make an Italian kingdom, but he did Italianize Amboise. He crowned the old fort with light, punching in the flower-peaked skylight and adding the fine Gothic gallery that opens on a balcony over the Loire. At right angles to the older residence, Charles's successors, those most Italianate majesties Louis XII and François I, added a new wing, adorning it with fine flanking turrets ornamented with sculpted dormers. But the Renaissance impulse did not push aside Amboise's warrior purpose. Leonardo da Vinci came here to die, but there was still a garrison under Louis XII.

Amboise figures in French history as the site of the denouement of the plot of the quiet captain. He was a certain La Reynaudie, a small-time Huguenot lord. He hatched a plot to eliminate the Guise brothers, the duke and the cardinal, leaders of the ultra-Catholic faction and principal *bêtes noires* of the Protestant interest as well as the complaisant king, François II, then at Blois. Amboise was easier to defend than Blois, so François fled here when he and the Guise got wind of Reynaudie's plans. Undeterred, the Huguenot gentlemen decided to attack in small, resolute bands who could use the element of surprise to force an entry to the fortress.

But betrayal dogs those who are loyal-to-conscience as well as those loyal-to-the-king. One of their own gave the

Huguenot plan away. The Guise attacked well north of Amboise at Château-Renault, killing the quiet captain and many of the men who had come from all over France to aid him. But the Catholics had won only a battle, not yet the war.

On March 19, 1560, Louis I de Bourbon, first Prince of Condé, uncle of the future Henry IV, and leader of the Protestant cause, brought the surviving Huguenots against Amboise. Win or lose, the prince was counting on some measure of success. If his forces prevailed, he was at their head; if they failed, he was in a position to soften the inevitable chastisement. The Catholics won the day. The brothers Guise were in no mood to use Condé's arithmetic and made a clean sweep. All the captives were condemned to death, with nobles decapitated on the terrace, and lesser conspirators hanged from the balcony over the Loire—the Balcony of the Plotters. Condé escaped his fellows' fate only by agreeing to soak his sword publicly in their blood.

The Renaissance elegance of Amboise never overcame the memory of that terrible day. When François II left the château, he was the last king to occupy it. It became a prison and welcomed several illustrious guests. The stern Colbert sent down superintendent of royal finances Nicolas Fouquet, patron of La Fontaine and Molière and builder of the palatial château of Vaux le Vicomte near Paris, to contemplate the folly of getting too rich in the royal service. The Sun King (Louis XIV) sent the amorous Duke of Lauzun to meditate the power of monarchical jealousy. Much later, Abd el-Kader, the emir of Algeria, pondered here the fate of kings after the final French conquest of that unfortunate land.

Leonardo da Vinci lived his last days at Amboise. His remains are housed in the elegant, Flamboyant Gothic St. Hubert Chapel.

The tympan above the central
door of the St. Hubert Chapel
depicts Charles VII, who was
born and died at Amboise, and
his wife, Anne of Brittany,
praying at the feet of the Virgin.

The noble hope of Valmer

The chalky vineyards of the delightful Vouvray wines wind down the banks of the River Brenne from Château-Renault in the north to the town of Vouvray on the Loire. Frothy Vouvrays have been valued high and sold dear since the fifteenth century, when they became favorites of the English.

A mayor of Tours, the bourgeois Jean Binet, built Valmer among the vines, a mere four leagues northeast of the city, in the early sixteenth century. A real notable had to offer his guests the best of the country. Social success was measured first and foremost in the depths of the wine barrel, so the aspiring mayor wanted his Vouvray available and deliverable to his home all the year through.

Land was a rung on the social ladder, and Vouvray land was also valued in vines-per-arpent and hogsheads sold. At harvest time, Binet made the trip to Tours frequently because its market transformed wine into solid profit. In the days when the kings were from Touraine, lending to the monarchical enterprise could produce royal returns.

Binet wasn't alone in turning his investment into present profit and noble prospect. The whole valley of the Brenne was dappled with charming little country seats like those of Launay and La Côte, and La Vallière at Reugny, dating from the sixteenth century. Behind the façade of each is a bourgeois financier or office holder. It seems as if the acquisition, and better yet, the construction of a château in Renaissance style had become a must by the beginning of the sixteenth century. A château, even one on which the turrets were just for show, was a first step toward a coat of arms and membership in the aristocracy.

Mayor Jean Binet never ceased to think of becoming Viscount or Baron Valmer. After all, another Jean, Jean Bourré—born as common as Binet at Château Gontier in 1424—had crossed the line into the Quality. Bourré had enriched himself in the Dauphin's service and risen to general comptroller of finances and first treasurer of France. He acquired many lordly châteaux, and his acquisitions had

ennobled him: the châteaux of Vau, Jarzé, and Plessis-Bourré figured in his arms. Valmer was to serve the same end for Jean Binet.

In Renaissance Tours, the financier and office-holder held the high ground, encouraging new industries such as silk and printing. Printers from Touraine like Mathieu Chercelé, Jean Rousset, and Camille Bourgeat were of European renown. The wealth and prestige of Tours and the nearness of the monarch stimulated the chase after taste and style. The rising men chose the best artists for the construction and decoration of their mansions. Binet rushed to ruin with light-giving dormers, charming small columns, and painted lintels. A pious man, he dug a chapel under Valmer, where others put their wine cellars. Despite his worldly wealth, he hoped to add heaven's grace to his fortune.

Splendid Italian-style gardens spread out and over Valmer's terraces.

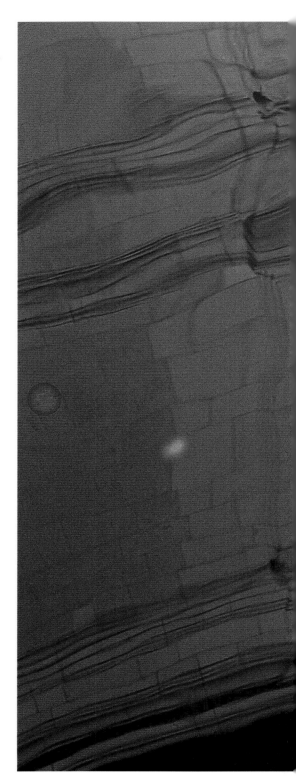

Built in 1536, Villandry was the last of the great Renaissance châteaux to grace the banks of the Loire.

The gardens of **Villandry**

Located at the confluence of the Cher and Loire, Villandry is the work of Jean Le Breton, prime contractor of the phantasmagoria at Chambord, secretary of state, and financier to François I.

Villandry has a slightly junior twin in the château at Villesavin, built by the masons who cut and stacked Chambord, and presented to Le Breton by François I in recognition of his zealous services as royal administrator and president of the court of audits for the county of Blois. Villesavin, erected in 1537, is one of the first clearly French Renaissance châteaux. Prefiguring the masterpiece at Fontainebleau, there are no towers and no closed courts; pavilions raised at right angles open onto a broad terrace. Begun in 1532 and finished in 1536 on the site of the ruined fortress of Combiers, where Capet Philippe II Augustus signed his victor's peace with Plantagent Henry II in 1189, the horseshoe-shaped residence of Villandry opens over the waters of the Loire and Cher.

The techniques of the French Renaissance architect are

plainly visible. Finely sculpted balconies crown each of the three connected buildings; porticoes of molded arches and pillars form a long gallery; elegant pilasters frame the stone window casements. Held within impressive sculpted frames, delicate mullions vein wide, light-shedding dormers. Clear-running water in the moats evoked the miraculous fishing of the little ports of the nearby Loire, where the fishermen cast their nets across the river from their longboats and brought up large quantities of shad and salmon.

The enormous vegetable garden—the *potager*—is spread over nine neatly square gardens, where each square is calculated to bring together plants whose colors please the eye as their fruits please the palate. In the ornamental gardens, the spray of water jets hang above reflecting pools in grandiose fountains and niches. Along the walks, embroideries of box trees and labyrinths of carefully tended hedges tease the mind.

The gardens lie on three broad levels beneath a hill dotted with arbors and planted with rare plant species. Parterres

The village and church seen from the château.

Villandry is celebrated for its gardens. The most original is its color-sensitive vegetable garden.

Above, from left to right: the vegetable garden in the Fall; the jardin d'amour; *a second view of the vegetable garden's autumnal splendor; the* jardin de musique.

The vegetable garden at Villandry is made up of nine square patches planted with vegetables forming geometrical designs. The harmonious shading and hues vary according to the season.

(Overleaf) Left, above and below: the jardin de musique; *at far right, above, the* jardin d'amour, *below, the vegetable garden.*

Right: the vegetable garden at the jardin des simples *for growing aromatics, medicinals, and condiments.*
Opposite: The jardin d'eau *with its jets and reflecting pools.*
*(*Overleaf*) The* jardin d'ornement *shaped with tightly clipped hedges and flowers.*

and terraces created by Androuet du Cerceau—first among French Renaissance architects and author in 1579 of the seminal *Plus Excellents Bâtiments de France*—made Villandry's garden the basic design of the new style, a foretaste of those at Fontainebleau and Versailles. In fact, Le Breton's Loire Valley classicism of pure and unencumbered line, symmetry in form, balance, and harmony precedes that of Paris.

In July 1639, Balthazar Le Breton, a descendant of Jean, became the Marquis of Villandry by letters patent, gaining the right to bear a coat of arms. Better late than never; the monarchy did sometimes know how to thank true benefactors of the realm. With Villandry and Villesavin, Jean Le Breton created the first of the great châteaux of the *Grand Siècle* to come. And at Villandry he presented France with the invaluable gift of the most extraordinary, the most original, and the loveliest French gardens.

The château of Sleeping Beauty: Ussé

With its turrets, towers, battlements, parapets, and spires so strongly medieval that they might be Disney simulations, Ussé rises from the marshy lands below the confluence of the rivers Indre and Loire. Once upon a time, the local peasants used the soggy fields to grow the hemp for the ropes of boats plying trade between Tours and Tuscany. Crossing the drawbridge one expects a murky prison, but one finds a splendid palace. Of course, Ussé's Gothic style is pure effect; the humanism is real.

Jacques d'Espinay was chamberlain to both Louis XI and Charles VIII. When he and his son Charles took possession, they thought the medieval keep erected by Antoine de Bueil too rough and tumble for the refined times of the later fifteenth century. So they constructed a Great House, a vast residence whose roofs turn toward the sun with many dormers and a façade that is resplendent with windows crowned with classical pediments and ornamented with a hundred graceful whims.

Ussé's new interior was worthy of both the light shining in

A medieval castle with the inevitable crenelated towers, Ussé was embellished with windows with classic pediments, dormers, and small turrets in the sixteenth century.

and the wealth of the d'Espinay. Son Charles was of a pious disposition, as well as an anxious patron of the arts. The chapel's sculpted prayer stalls, Aubusson tapestries with their classical stories, the Tuscan triptych set in gold, and the ceramic Virgin by the Florentine sculptor Lucca della Robbia—all are his devoted work. To make that clear, he had his name and that of his wife, Lucrèce de Pons, elegantly carved into the walls.

In the seventeenth century, legend said that a young princess lay enchanted behind Ussé's massy walls. Charles Perrault, who was a comptroller general for construction in the reign of Louis XIV as well as a collector of old tales, made the legend famous in his story of *Sleeping Beauty*. From outside Ussé, the involvement of a wicked witch does not seem farfetched. From inside, protracted somnolence seems perfectly feasible. Well, perhaps it *is* unlikely that a sensible young woman would sleep here a hundred years. On the other hand, a marriage-minded, handsome prince does not often waken a princess with a kiss. The inconvenience would not obtrude as it might in a lesser place. And the chapel decor ensured that nuptials would reflect a proper delicacy.

Louis Bernin de Valentinay, comptroller general for the Sun King's household, had a son who might very well have passed for a handsome prince. In 1691, Valentinay *fils* wed the daughter of the great fortress builder Vauban, uniting the transient to the eternal. We are assured that the fiancé did not first put his "princess" to sleep so as to emulate the legend, and the marriage did take place at Ussé. It was a worthy ceremony. The wedding party—a magnificent parade of notables in perukes—proceeded gaily down the terraces and through the groves and arbors of the ornamental garden to the banks of the Indre. The tale of it reached an admiring Versailles; the young de Valentinay must have done well at court, for the king created their marquisate in 1701.

Ussé has made a long career as a château of legend. It sat Chateaubriand at the feet of the Duchess of Duras—a worthy place made for encounters of the literary type.

Built on the waters and in the Italian style, Azay-le-Rideau leaves behind the French Gothic tradition for good and all.

The graces of Azay-le-Rideau

Azay-le-Rideau. The ancient land of France—the Touraine—began with the towns and châteaux between the rivers Indre and Loire. The places are so many acts in the succeeding national dramas, and their names are the sounds of good old French—Luynes, Cinq-Mars, Langeais, Villandry, Valmer, Montbazon, and Azay.

Azay was the stage for one crucial act. In 1415, the battle at Agincourt made the English crossbowman master of France. In 1418, the Burgundians, English allies, seized Azay. The dauphin Charles, now only the kinglet of a small province, was making his way from Chinon to Tours. As he passed under Azay's walls toward the stone bridge on the Indre, the jeers and taunts of the insolent Burgundians filled the air. They did not go unanswered. The Dauphin and his men took the place by assault, put the Burgundians to the sword, and the town to the torch.

For the kings of France, Azay became a synonym for victory. It received and long kept a new name: Azay-le-Brulé—Azay the Burnt. But the bridge lent the town strategic

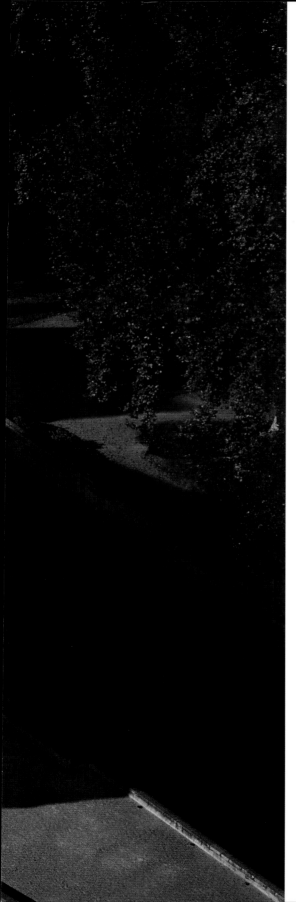

Azay-le-Rideau is one of the first châteaux where the symmetry of the façade imposes itself over the whole.

value, so the little king of Bourges was quick to allow the remaining citizens to rebuild the town and fortress. Both were important gauges of a teetering monarchy's survival— the town for its commerce, the fortress for its strength.

By the beginning of the sixteenth century, the good old land had slipped into peace and prosperity. Its rich soil was thick with coveted wine grapes. Tours had become a grand capital, host to a thriving silk industry and a bourgeoisie with money to lend and a royal government anxious to borrow it. Gilles Berthelot, treasurer of France and mayor of Tours, was a man of his times. Of considerable wealth and admirable taste, he bought the Azay fortress as a sort of summer house or hunting rendezvous.

From 1518 to 1529, Gilles rebuilt the rough castle in the Italian style, anchoring one part in the Indre's bed and the other in the sweet green of the forest. Despite the château's severe and soaring slate roofs, monumental fireplaces, and rounded towers, the Gothic style was definitively banished. The white local stone became a part of the architect's aesthetic vision. Light is let in, but honored also with shaped stone casements and sculpted dormers. The great quadrilateral is pinned at its four corners by small turrets with tightly sloped roofs. The grand central staircase within became Azay's structural and moral focus. Its four grand landings are twinned bays profuse with graces: canopied alcoves, pilasters, friezes embroidered with arabesques, tiny columns, dormers. Balzac wrote of Azay-le-Rideau as being "a diamond polished on every face, masked with flowers, mounted on piles, and set in the Indre."

All the work that Gilles did has been branded with the salamander and stoat totems of King François I and his Queen Claude. In those days, money-lending could be as dangerous as soldiering. A financier might quite suddenly find himself guilty of embezzlement. Worse, his wealth might very well convict him of *lèse majesté*. In 1527, the erstwhile royal banker and lord of Semblançay, Jacques de Beaune, made a hasty trip to the gibbet for corruption. But no honest man had pointed the finger at Jacques, so it was necessary to root out his accomplices. Downriver at Montrésor, Imbert de Bastarnay trembled and installed his tomb in the chapel. Gilles made a rapid flight toward the horizon, taking refuge at Metz, which was German at the time. He died an exile.

With Gilles out of the way, François made Azay his own and it became a royal *pied à terre*. Louis XIII definitely stayed here during his lifetime, 1610–1643. Perhaps his son, Louis XIV, did too. And why not? The royal offices of the good city of Tours surely furnished Azay's honest bourgeois comforts in the first place.

The southern and eastern façades are reflected in the broad pools that replaced the ancient moats.

At home with Balzac: Saché

Saché gets its fame second hand. The laurels belong to the nineteenth-century novelist Honoré de Balzac—a sort of Trollopian Dickens—who shut himself up here to write. Balzac was a native son, a Tourangeau, who sited his novels in the Loire. *Père Goriot*, set at Saumur, springs to mind. No doubt he found inspiration here for his *Lys dans la vallée*, based on his boarding-school days in Vendôme, in the gardens of the park. Saché is just one among many old Renaissance châteaux-cum-country houses dotting the valley of the River Indre. The château's nineteenth-century owners made profound changes that do not merit even a footnote in an architectural digest. The enormously fat Balzac stretched his rare walks to include the charming church. Its square bell tower recalls feudal times and the Masses said before and after twelfth-century battles. Inside, the delicate arches webbing the vaults recall the perpetual delights of life in the Loire Valley.

Saché, whose fame rests upon Balzac's literary accomplishments, has a lovely park on the banks of the River Indre.

Chinon *and the Plantagenets*

The vast expanse of Chinon spreads along the banks of the
River Vienne just below its confluence with the Loire. Through
the early Middle Ages it was a march of the realm, sharply
disputed during four centuries of English and French rivalry
on French soil. So, although at the heart of France, this part
of the realm bears more of English history than French in its
stones and legends. Henry II Plantagenet, his wife Eleanor of
Aquitaine, their son Richard the Lion-Hearted, and daughter-
in-law Isabelle of Angoulême, widow of Henry's other son,
King John Lackland of Robin Hood fame, have their tombs at
the Abbey of Fontevraud, about fourteen miles from this great
fortress. Chinon was the principal stronghold against the
incursions of English soldiers moving from Aquitaine up the
Vienne or from Richelieu in the Poitou, the ancient province
that came to the English crown through Eleanor.

Interestingly, Rabelais—and with him, Gargantua and
Pantagruel—is a native son. The land is rich in vines, wines,
and forest game. Its history predates and postdates the
Plantagenet-Capet rivalry. Celts held the heights of Chinon

village, then Gauls, and then Romans, who first made it a fortified town before the present great fortress began to take shape in the tenth century. The surrounding countryside brims with châteaux, ranging from the Gothic Le Riveau along the road to Chatellerault in the south to Ussé at the entry of the great Chinon forest. Above the Loire are the great military works at Saumur, and below, those of Montsoreau.

Constructed on a limestone spur overlooking the river valley, the fortress of Chinon is really three castles built over the site of the Roman town. The first was Fort St. Georges, which now lies in glorious ruin on the doorstep of the Pavillon de l'Horloge of the Château du Milieu, which was the second to be built. Fort St. Georges was named by Henry Plantagenet to honor the patron saint of England. The Pavillon's clock—called Marie-Javelle—rings out the hours at this tragic place. At Fort St. Georges, on July 7, 1189, Henry learned of the treason committed by his sons Richard and John, who took arms against him, and he died of heartbreak. Upon hearing the news, Richard hurried to his father's bier. The paternal

curse lay on the faithless son: Henry's corpse was bleeding from the nose. Ten years later, wounded in the shoulder by a crossbow, Richard came here to plead for the intercession of St. George at Henry's chapel and died.

Frequented by the kings of France and England from the twelfth to the fourteenth centuries, the Château du Milieu is no less medieval than Fort St. Georges. Even though it is set behind deep moats and flanked by strong towers, this building is not devoid of comforts. Within is the throne room where, on March 9, 1429, Joan of Arc first saw the Dauphin among his courtiers. When the Dauphin, with Joan's help, became Charles VII, he had his residence linked to the little manor of Roberdeau by an underground passage to facilitate his trysts with his beloved and beautiful Agnès Sorel. The court was happy at Chinon. After all, beneath its stony gaze, the hills brimmed with the blessed vineyards.

Fort du Coudray is the third castle. It possesses an exceptionally strong keep whose bleakness recalls grim times. In the thirteenth century Philippe le Bel IV imprisoned

Chinon, a bulwark of the Loire Valley, held the marches of a hotly disputed realm for four centuries.

Chinon comprises three castles—Fort St. Georges, Château du Milieu, and Fort du Coudray, which are separated one from the other by defensive ditches.

there Jacques de Molay and his too-powerful Templars. A highly politicized trial—still notable for its bad faith—was held. De Molay was led up to Paris to be burned at the stake on the Place de Grève, with his face to the East, where the crusading order had made its fortune.

English history in France surely began with Eleanor of Aquitaine, the queen of two enemy kings. Plantagenet Henry II was Eleanor's second husband, her first having been Capet Louis VII. Probably it's shared history; better still, it's universal history.

Glittering Réaux

The château of Les Réaux rises from the northern slope of the Loire between the towns of Saumur and Langeais in the valley of kings. Jean Briçonnet, mayor of Tours, built its checkerboard façade of brick and limestone, towers, and turrets on the ruined walls of the older stronghold of Plessis-Rideau, from which, until the seventeenth century, it took its name. Jean supplied the ring of moats. The original Plessis was constructed in 1385, while the present building went up in 1435. For a little while, Plessis belonged to Antoine de Bueil, husband to Jeanne de France, the legitimized daughter of Charles VII and his mistress Agnès Sorel.

The golden age of Plessis came in the Sun King's time. Gédéon Tallemant, whose memoir *Historiettes du grand siècle* has long spiced up the bibliography of the period, bought the place from a descendant of the Briçonnet family. Much in favor at Louis XIV's perfumed court, Tallemant obtained the right to call Plessis "Les Réaux," a name derived from the French plural of the Spanish word "real," the traditional gold piece. Gédéon's formal name, Tallemant des Réaux, as well as his little checkerboard *pied à terre*, speak of his hopes, his means, and his success.

The red-and-white checkerboard façade of Les Réaux.

Candes-Saint-Martin is a
defensive stronghold built at the
crossroads of the rivers Loire
and Vienne.

Candes-Saint-Martin

Candes-Saint-Martin occupies a defensive site on the western
slope of the Loire, just above its confluence with the River
Vienne. The little town dug into the sparkly tufa huddles at
the feet of a great squat abbey church. Saint Martin rules
here. A miracle worker, a dowser of miraculous waters,
Martin lent his name to the abbey at Tours, the wealthiest in
Rome's Three Gauls.

Near the end of the fifteenth century, with the wars of
religion raging, the archbishops of Tours, worried for the
safety of their worldly treasures, turned their eyes upon
Candes, which the Gauls had founded as a fortified village.
It seemed to be a suitable site, so they erected keep,
battlements, and parapets, along with a lovely flower garden
and a comfortable residence on the higher ground above the
abbey. Near the end of the seventeenth century, Louis XIV
revoked the Edict of Nantes and his dragoons became
missionaries to the Huguenots. Archbishop Michel Armelot de
Gourmay erected a second castle. This was soon demolished,
but was rebuilt by a certain Cailleau, mayor of Angers, in the
cash-strapped twilight of the *ancien régime*.

La dame de Montsoreau

La Dame de Montsoreau by Alexandre Dumas outraged history to immortalize the château. His heroine, Diane de Maridor, the tragic lady of the title, was based on Françoise de Chambes. Her husband, Charles de Chambes, the Count of Montsoreau, did indeed kill her lover, Louis de Clermont de Bussy d'Amboise. Not at Montsoreau, but at the little manor of Coutancière. With the spat so thoroughly settled, the couple supposedly made up their differences and went on with their lives.

The Loire's chalky slopes are riddled with deep caves where humans have doubtless lived in times out of mind, and the valuable local wines have long been stored. Montsoreau still abides as a medieval river fortress watching the southern bank just below the junction of the River Vienne. Its face to the Loire is all crenellation, loophole, and machicolation for the discharge of stones and spears, arrows and boiling oil. Covered parapets link massive square towers. The drawbridge is well flanked, the walls around slick and thick. Montsoreau symbolized strategy as well as tactics; the bridge below is the key to the Chinon region and points south.

Medieval does not mean dungeon-like. In 1455, Jean de Chambes, a lord with a taste for comfortable living, began the process that would lead from castle to châteauhood. A counselor to Charles VII during the expulsion of the English, Jean was more diplomat than warrior, but his domain nonetheless became a barony in 1560 and a county in 1573. Barony or county, the château of Montsoreau played no role in the assassination of Louis de Clermont de Bussy d'Amboise, a grisly character, to be sure, and no friend of the de Chambes. He distinguished himself in the 1572 St. Bartholomew's Day Massacre by taking the opportunity to murder a relative, with whom he happened to be involved in a lawsuit, with his own hand. The Duke of Anjou named Louis commandant of Angers, the capital of his province. He took the opportunity to pillage it. But he definitely did not, in spite of Dumas's words, seduce the wife of Jean de Chambes. It was the wife of Charles de Chambes, Jean's brother.

From the outside, Dumas's massy, grim, and menacing Montsoreau is apt. Once the drawbridge is crossed, it is less so. The elegantly decorated spiral staircase immediately evokes the sweetness of the Renaissance. The de Chambes seem to have loved the painters and sculptors of the Loire Valley. The mounting column of the ceremonial staircase, added in 1520, leads to four floors of windows framed in sculpted motifs separated by bas reliefs. It terminates beneath a great palm-shaped vault, that is most elegantly arched. For decoration, painted monkeys work in a quarry where they raise the blocks to the surface with a pulley.

Although Dumas was sloppy with his facts, the dramatic core of *La Dame de Montsoreau* is not just heedless fantasy. Many are the tales of public and private violence of the good old times at Montsoreau, and it was common enough for a jealous lord to kill a lover, and lovers of rich baronesses were particularly susceptible. Civil wars in France, as in England, multiplied the number of the tragically widowed because their husbands were also dying. In the late fifteenth century, not far from Montsoreau and on the road between Dampierre and Souzay, a discreet manor sheltered Marguerite of Anjou, one so widowed. The daughter of the exiled poet René the Good, Duke of Anjou, formerly king of sunny Naples, Marguerite passed her days in the shadow of death. She had lost both her husband, Lancaster Henry VI of England, and her son to an assassin during the War of the Roses.

Saumur squats over the more ancient
defensive tunnels and caves clawed
out of the living rock.

The ramparts of Saumur

From behind a broad slope and a ring of moats, Saumur's thick walls soar high above the surrounding dolmens and menhirs. The place has certainly been the refuge of threatened populations from prehistoric times. The Gauls used it, then the Romans. When the Vikings thrust up the rivers cutting peasant throats as they came, Saumur was still a blessed site honeycombed with tunnels leading to vast caves where refugees could shelter out of range of the marauder's torch.

Located on a rocky promontory just above the confluence of the little River Thouet and the Loire, it is impossible to move upriver out of Angers and on to Tours without passing Saumur, so the stronghold at Saumur became the sentinel of what would become the royal province of Touraine. Thibault the Swindler, Count of Blois, is the first-known contributor to the present fortress in the tenth century. Feudal lords of Thibault's hardy strain carried on the work until the dukes of Anjou came into possession. After Eleanor of Aquitaine's

marriage to Henry Plantagenet, the fortress fell into the hands of the kings of England, but soon returned to French hands, which never again let it fall. Not once during the whole course of the Hundred Years War were the English able to take it.

Saumur's eleventh-century keep is of huge cut stones that seem to grow from the natural rock. In the twelfth and thirteenth centuries, the keep was complemented with one and then another castle. The present building was reconstructed, completed, and hesitantly embellished in the second half of the fourteenth century by Duke Louis of Anjou, brother to King Charles V the Wise, and it has remained as it mostly was in the age of chivalry.

Everything was done to make Saumur safe for man and beast. Four polygonal towers that rise off round bases mark due north, west, south, and east. These were once tied together by thick, strongly buttressed walls topped by a covered parapet walk equipped with watchtowers and machicolation at intervals. Pointed towers soared off the southern wall, facing the English lands. The small, castle-like

Constructed on the foundations of an earlier fortress, today's château of white tufa was completed and reworked in the second half of the fifteenth century.

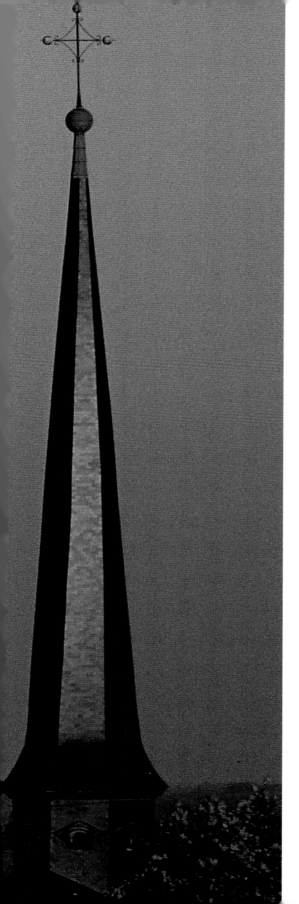

Left: Saumur is a quadrilateral with a high tower at each of the four cardinal points of the compass.
(Overleaf) *From its promontory, the château dominates the town it once so faithfully protected.*

main entry gives onto a broad, square courtyard. All was well-suited to withstand a siege. A great cistern held rainwater. Storehouses allowed for stockpiling.

At the end of the Hundred Years War, René, the poet Duke of Anjou, found Duke Louis's work just a bit too sober and resolved to brighten it up and make it livable. At one end of the main residence, a turret already adorned a grand staircase decorated with canopied alcoves and lit by bays. René decided to add another at the other end, installed fireplaces throughout, tiled the floors, and hung tapestries decorated with mythical scenes.

Throughout the Middle Ages, Saumur's massive pile had always saved the people. In the seventeenth century, the people's loyalty saved the massive pile. Richelieu chose it as his headquarters when he set about razing the Protestant redoubts in the Loire, Saumur was spared by its service to the community. Later, Cardinal Mazarin and the regent, Anne of Austria, chose royalist Saumur for their headquarters when they liquidated the noble rebels holed up at Angers.

La Roche-aux-Moines

The château of Roche-aux-Moines dominates the Serrant, the rich and rolling promised land of the Angevin *blancs-de-blancs*. There is also etymological irony, for the root *serre* in Provençale means "low hill," in Latin, "bolt, lock," and in French tourist, "squeeze."

It is said that in the second century the Breton knight Buart presented the rocky little hill to the monks of the Abbey of St. Nicholas of Angers, hence the name Monks Hill. But no such place name appears before the thirteenth century. In 1310, a siege castle was built on the site and the seneschal Guillaume des Roches held sway. The seneschal had no clerical pretensions whatsoever.

In 1370, Duke Louis II of Anjou bought the castle from Guillaume's heir, Guillaume de Craon, and the place became the Roche-au-Duc. In the fifteenth century, Pontus de Brie arrived there; he was a crony of Louis XI and lord of the Serrant. Pontus named his new château Roche de Serrant. However, the locals much preferred the name Roche-aux-Moines in memory of the monks who brought the happy vine—that "plant de vigne de Baume"—and fortune to the Serrant from Duke Louis's Burgundian domains.

Roche-aux-Moines dominates the Serrant, the promised land of the blanc-de-blancs.

Landscape painting: The Château du Pin

A small fortress was erected on the site in the twelfth century. Ruined in the course of the fourteenth-century Breton wars, it was soon rebuilt. The square keep sheltering the stone staircase dates from the same period.

The charm of the medieval Château du Pin is nature and nurture rather than stone: the careful profusion of hundred-year-old limes, shaped shrubberies, delphiniums, yellow roses, and parterres of iris. The chestnut trees growing in the dry moats are four hundred years old. At the foot of the park, lush green water meadows—flooded when the Loire runs high—line the banks of the little river. The Château du Pin brings medieval splendor into some of the most romantic country decor anywhere.

The lovely gardens lend comeliness to the brick and stone of Château du Pin.

The chapel seen from a parterre
of iris.

The Loire Valley

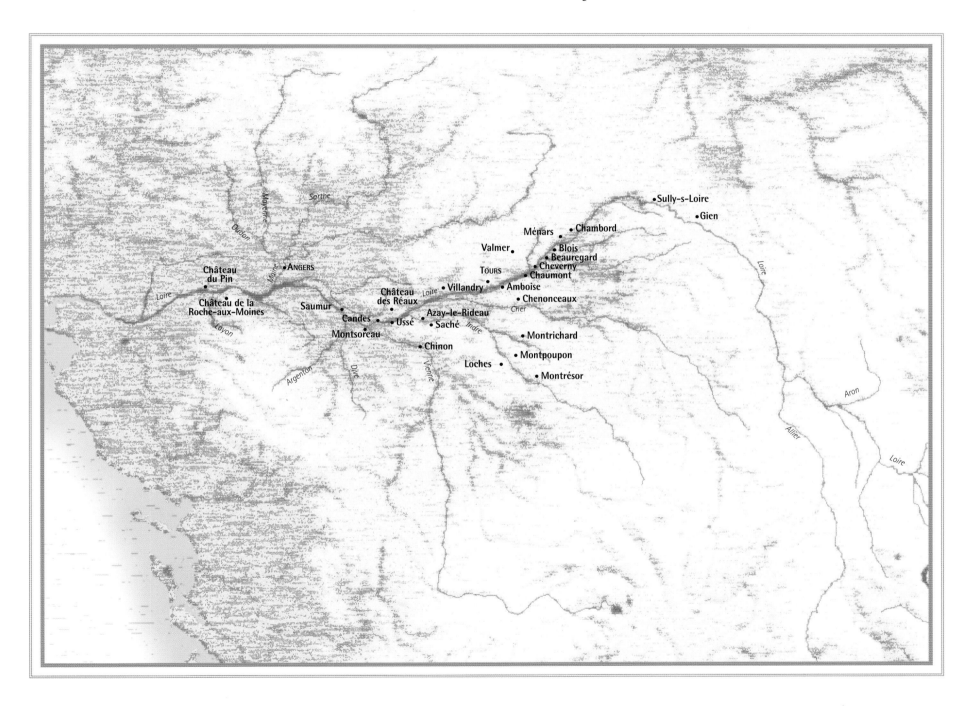

Acknowledgments

Jean-Baptiste Leroux owes a debt of gratitude for the kindness of
the many owners and curators of the châteaux photographed for
this book.

Photographs by Leroux are distributed by the Hoa-Qui agency.
Photographs were taken using Fujichrome Velvia film. The
photographer wishes to thank Société Hasselblad France and
Philippe Lachot of Photo-Denfert for their help in bringing the book
to fruition.

The chefs Jean-Claude Rigollet at Chinon and Ghislaine Sallé at
Neuilly-Le-Lierre, whose aid was, admittedly, *hors d'oeuvre*, merit
an appreciative nod and wink.

PENGUIN STUDIO
Published by the Penguin Group
Penguin Putnam Inc., 375 Hudson Street,
New York, New York 10014, U.S.A.

Penguin Books Ltd, 27 Wrights Lane,
London W8 5TZ, England

Penguin Books Australia Ltd, Ringwood,
Victoria, Australia

Penguin Books Canada Ltd, 10 Alcorn Avenue
Toronto, Ontario, Canada M4V 3B2

Penguin Books (N.Z.) Ltd, 182-90 Wairau Road,
Auckland 10, New Zealand

Penguin Books Ltd, Registered Offices:
Harmondsworth, Middlesex, England

First published in the United States by Penguin Studio,
a member of Penguin Putnam Inc.

First Printing, July 1999
10 9 8 7 6 5 4 3 2 1

Library of Congress Catalog Number: 99-70251

Book Design: Laurent Picard & Estève Gili.
Photo Engraving: Offset Publicité, Maison-Alfort.
Printed in Switzerland by Weber.
Bound in France by SMRF.

ISBN: 0-670-88644-0